The United Methodist Story

EDITORIAL AND DESIGN TEAM

Crystal A. Zinkiewicz
Anthony E. Peterson
Development Editors
Joy W. Thompson
Production Editor

J. S. Laughbaum
Cover Designer
Phillip D. Francis
Interior Layout Designer

ADMINISTRATIVE TEAM

Neil M. Alexander
Publisher
Harriett Jane Olson
Vice President

Duane A. Ewers
Executive Editor,
Teaching and Study Resources
M. Steven Games
Senior Editor of Youth Resources

THIS BOOK IS PRINTED ON RECYCLED PAPER

ISBN-0-687-72796-0

07—10 9 8

John Wesley

Contents

Introduction

If someone asked, "Who are you?" you would probably begin with your name, and then perhaps go on to describe where you live and where you go to work or school.

What if the question came again: "Who are you?" Then you might talk about your family and your cultural heritage, your interests and hobbies, and your plans for the future. Eventually, you might reveal some of your deepest feelings about life, about your relationships, about God.

To truly know who you are, another person must learn about every facet of your one-of-a-kind personality. What you look like, your family, your likes and dislikes, your most private feelings—all make you unique and irreplaceable.

Background

How would you respond if someone asked, "Who are United Methodists?" Just as you are unique, so is our church. Just as your past, your family, and your experiences have shaped you, so have the last three centuries shaped Methodism. To know what it means to be a United Methodist, it's important to learn about the church's history, its beliefs, and its place in the world.

So who are we? Where do we come from? What makes us different from Roman Catholics, or Baptists, or Presbyterians? To a large degree, it's our history that makes us unique. United Methodists have an amazing family tree, over two hundred years old and still growing. All the women and men who have gone before us are part of our family tree. Like each of us, they questioned and doubted and struggled with the challenges of living their faith in the real world. Because of them, we United Methodists have a distinctive way of looking at our relationship with God and our responsibilities in the world.

And it all began in the heart and mind of one man. His name was John Wesley.

Background of the "Methodist" Family of Churches in the United States

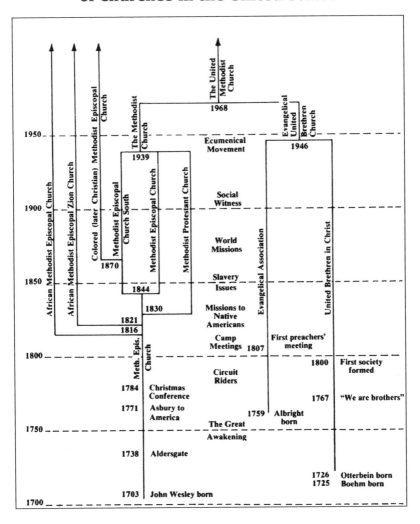

© 1975 United Methodist Communications

Chapter 1

John and Charles Wesley: How Should Christians Live?

John Wesley grew up in an isolated, small town called Epworth, in England. Born in 1703, he had two brothers and seven sisters; nine other children died as babies. His father, Samuel, was pastor of the town's Anglican (Church of England) parish. His mother, Susanna, ran her large household with a firm but loving hand. She taught all the children to read and write, and was their first spiritual teacher as well. She spent private time every week with each child, talking with him or her about God. Susanna taught her children to have a disciplined life. They were not to waste any time that could be spent learning, worshiping, or helping others.

Samuel and Susanna Wesley

When John was six years old, the family's home was destroyed by fire in the middle of the night. In the confusion, little Jacky was left behind in his bedroom. When they realized he was still in the house, his father and several neighbors formed a human ladder and grabbed him from a second-floor window. Later in life, John Wesley referred to himself as a "brand plucked from the burning," based on Amos 4:11. His mother later wrote that she would "be more particularly careful of the soul . . . that [God] hast so mercifully provided for," and that she would work "to instil into his mind the disciplines of thy true religion and virtue" (as quoted in *Reasonable Enthusiast*, by Henry D. Rack; Abingdon Press, 1992; page 57). Jacky learned his lessons well.

As a young man John attended Oxford University, where he and his younger brother Charles led a small group of students who wanted to practice their faith more actively. They prayed together, studied the Bible, and earnestly discussed their innermost spiritual concerns. They collected food for the poor and visited prisoners in the local jail. They kept detailed diaries, noting their activities and their spiritual conditions for almost every hour of the day. Some people made fun of them, calling them "the Holy Club" and "Bible Moths" (because they spent so much time "fluttering" around the Bible). They were also called "Methodists" because they approached their faith in such a methodical way—and that's the name that stuck.

John and Charles followed in their father's footsteps and became ordained pastors (called priests) in the Church of England. After several years of preaching and teaching, however, John was frustrated in his spiritual walk. He longed to be closer to God, to have more confidence in his own salvation. In 1735, when he was thirty-two years old, a way opened that he thought would help him achieve that confidence; it led across the Atlantic Ocean to the colony of Georgia.

The American colony of Georgia had been established by English investors as a home for the "worthy poor." One of the leaders in its establishment was General James Oglethorpe. John persuaded his brother that they should offer themselves in service to the colony, and they were accepted. Charles was named secretary to General Oglethorpe and pastor of the settlement at Frederica. John was to be pastor to the settlement at Savannah and he also planned to be a missionary to the Indians. He had high hopes that as he exposed the Native Americans to the Christian faith, his own faith would be deepened and strengthened.

That's not how it worked out. Neither brother had a good experience in Georgia. Charles had some conflicts with Oglethorpe and with the settlers, and he just wasn't suited to deal with all the paperwork generated by his job. On top of all that, he became ill; so he returned to England (in 1736) after a few months.

For his part, John was opposed by many of the colonists, who were not very interested in his strict methods of religious observance. He rarely got the chance to preach to the Indians; and even when he did, they were not nearly as receptive to his preaching as he had hoped they would be. He fell in love with a young woman, but couldn't decide whether to marry her. When she married someone else, he felt hurt and angry.

But most of all, John struggled with his spiritual condition. He followed all the rules, obeyed the church's teachings, read his Bible, prayed, and did good works. Why, then, did he not feel closer to God?

On the ship to Georgia, he had met a group of Christians called Moravians, who almost glowed with the love of God. Why didn't he have their inner assurance of God's loving presence in their lives? When the ship nearly sank in a terrible storm, the Moravians awed him with their unshakable faith in God.

John Wesley

In despair in Georgia, John Wesley wrote, "I went to America, to convert the Indians; but oh, who shall convert me?"

He finally gave up on Georgia after nearly two years. At the age of thirty-five, John Wesley returned to England. He was discouraged by his experience in America, and shaken and puzzled by the joyful witness of the Moravians. Several months later, still discouraged, he went to a prayer meeting on Aldersgate Street in London. There he had an experience of God's love that made him feel connected to God in a way he never had felt before. He wrote in his journal, "I felt my heart strangely warmed. I felt I did trust in Christ, Christ alone for salvation; and an assurance was given me that He had taken away *my* sins, even *mine*, and saved *me* from the law of sin and death."

The Aldersgate experience, as United Methodists call it, triggered a change in John Wesley's life. While this event didn't free him from doubts, it marked a new direction in his life. His careful, methodical cultivation of Christlike behavior was now partnered with the heartwarming assurance that God loved him. Each reinforced the other; and Wesley soon began preaching this message to eager listeners, stressing both themes: that God's abundant love and grace is available to everyone, and that every Christian is called to live a disciplined life of holiness.

Charles Wesley, John's brother, had a similar experience of God's love just a few days before John's Aldersgate experience. Like John, Charles preached the Methodist message; but, more importantly, he used music to express himself. He wrote thousands of hymns during his lifetime. Many of them are still well known today, and they speak of God's love and of holy living in ways that ordinary people can understand and remember. Even

Charles Wesley

though the language is from the eighteenth century, the truth these hymns convey is timeless.

Here's how Charles Wesley expresses the Methodist idea that God's free grace is available to everyone: "Come, sinners, to the gospel feast, let every soul be Jesus' guest" (*The United Methodist Hymnal*, 616). And he answers the question, What does it mean to live a holy life? with these words: "I want a principle within of watchful, godly fear, a sensibility of sin, a pain to feel it near. . . . Almighty God of truth and love, to me thy power impart" (the *Hymnal*, 410).

The Wesley brothers began traveling from town to town, preaching to anyone who would listen. Preaching anywhere other than in a church was unusual in those days; but the Wesleys went where the people were: the

9

main street of a town, a farmer's field, or a seaside dock. Often they stood and sang hymns until a crowd had gathered, and then spoke from their hearts about God's transforming love and the joy of holy living.

Who were the people drawn to John Wesley's preaching? They were all ages from teenagers to

Crowd listening to John Wesley

older persons, both women and men; ordinary people: farmers, miners, housewives, and shopkeepers. Methodists usually were not wealthy, or fashionable, or powerful. Many of them had very hard lives, harder than we can imagine. Just keeping a roof over their head and food on the table was an everyday struggle. They found joy and hope in the preaching they heard. They found support and strength in the Wesleyan message of grace and holy living.

The Wesleys soon found others who wanted to preach their message. Usually men, they were sometimes pastors in the Church of England, but sometimes laypeople, too. Some laywomen also felt called to preach; and they, too, traveled from town to town, preaching, teaching, and organizing people into "societies," spreading the word to their neighbors about Methodism's message of God's freely-given love and forgiveness.

Being a Methodist in those days took courage. Some people ridiculed them for their "methodical" way of holy living, for acting as if there was more to being a Christian than simply going to church on Sunday. Some people did more than ridicule. They threw rotten fruit or stones at the preachers. Sometimes mobs chased them right out of town. Why? Probably because they didn't like the preachers telling them not to drink or gamble. They didn't like being told that they were sinners in need of salvation.

Yet there were many who did respond to the call for repentance, and the Wesleys' renewal movement kept right on growing. In fact, it grew so much that the borders of England couldn't hold it.

Chapter 2

Francis Asbury: Spreading the Good News in a New Land

Some of those working people who followed the Methodist way decided to join thousands of others seeking a new life in the American colonies. Just as today's immigrants to the United States are cut off from family, friends, and familiar landscapes, so were those early immigrants.

One little band of immigrants arrived together. Barbara Heck came with her cousin Philip Embury and a few other relatives to New York from Ireland. Philip, a layperson, had been a Methodist preacher in Ireland, but once in America devoted all of his time to his work as a carpenter. Barbara became concerned that no one was keeping to the Methodist way of living and worshiping. She confronted her cousin and urged him to start preaching

Francis Asbury

again. Because of her energies and his preaching, a small Methodist society formed in New York.

Farther south in Maryland, another Irish Methodist immigrant, Robert Strawbridge, began preaching to his neighbors. All over the colonies, small groups of Methodists started coming together; and soon the call went back to England: "Send us preachers!" Wesley heard the call, and sent missionaries to the growing American flock. One of those missionaries was named Francis Asbury.

Francis Asbury was a generation younger than John Wesley. He became a Methodist when he was sixteen, and two years later joined the ranks of Wesley's preachers. When Wesley called for volunteers to go to America, twenty-six-year-old Asbury stepped forward. He never looked back. He said good-bye to his parents and his friends, and followed God's call across the Atlantic Ocean.

The journey by ship took nearly eight weeks. A few days into his trip, Asbury wrote in his diary, "Whither am I going? To the New World. What to do? To gain honour? No, if I know my own heart. To get money? No; I am going to live to God, and to bring others so to do" (from *The Journal and Letters of Francis Asbury*, edited by Elmer T. Clark; Epworth Press and Abingdon Press, 1958; page 4). And that is exactly what he did for the next forty-five years.

Asbury loved his new home and traveled almost every mile of it, bringing the good news to people. He rode horseback over mountains, waded through rivers, and kept going in the worst weather and over the roughest terrain. He described one journey in his diary on March 28, 1793, when he was forty-seven years old:

"We made an early start, and came to the Beaver Dam [in western North Carolina]; three years ago we slept here in a cabin without a cover. We made a breakfast at Mr. W_____'s; and then attempted the iron or stone mountain, which is steep like the roof of a house. I found it difficult and trying to my lungs to walk up it. Descending the mountain, we had to jump down the steep stairs, from two to three and four feet. . . . We came down the river, where there are plenty of large, round, rolling stones, and the stream was rapid. My horse began to grow dull: an intermittent fever and a deep cold disordered me much" (from *The Journal and Letters of Francis Asbury*; pages 752–753).

The consecration of Francis Asbury

Asbury never had his own home, but lived on the road, staying with settlers or in public inns wherever he traveled. He became one of the most well-known people in America, simply because he traveled the length and breadth of the new country.

And Asbury did much more than preach. He became the leader of the American Methodist movement, and in many ways designed the church we have today. In 1784, after the end of the Revolutionary War, American Methodists broke away from their English parent (the Church of England) and formed their own separate church, The Methodist Episcopal Church. Francis Asbury became the first bishop of the new church.

Asbury's genius was in the way that he guided the church to respond to the needs of the growing country. Wesley's preachers in both England and America didn't stay in one place; rather, they rode "circuits" of several settlements, preaching in a different place every day. This method was perfectly suited to America, with its small scattered settlements on the frontier. Asbury didn't want Methodist preachers to stay in any one place too long;

after all, just down the road there might be someone who had never heard about God's saving love.

Some of Asbury's preachers found him autocratic, assigning them where they didn't want to go and firmly enforcing church discipline. He didn't apologize for that, because he felt that the future of Methodism depended on decisive and committed leadership. Under his firm hand, the Methodist movement spread like wildfire, especially on the frontier: places like Kentucky, Ohio, and Michigan.

Asbury assigned the Methodist preachers to large circuits, sometimes hundreds of miles long, which meant that the Methodists in any given community might not see their pastor more than one Sunday in three or four months. The laypeople had to take responsibility for keeping the church alive, just as they had in England. And just as it had in England, Methodism in America grew because of the commitment of laywomen and laymen.

Besides meeting on Sundays and in small groups, by the early nineteenth century there was a new way to worship God: the camp meeting. Methodists weren't the only ones to use the camp meeting, but they were the church most closely identified with it. Francis Asbury felt that camp meetings were responsible for thousands joining the Methodist fold. The camp meeting was a lively, colorful event lasting for several days. A farmer might allow people to meet in one of his fields, or a large space would be cleared in the woods. Hundreds, sometimes thousands, of people traveled for miles to the site. There several preachers took turns preaching and calling people to repent of their sins and accept Jesus as their Savior.

Camp meetings in the early years were far from quiet. Life in frontier areas was rough, and the people who lived there were hard-working, plain-spoken, and down-to-earth. There were no luxury hotels or air-conditioned auditoriums. The women slept in the wagons, and the men under the wagons. Music was a big part of the camp meeting. Hymns like "Alas! and Did My Savior Bleed" (*The United Methodist Hymnal,* 294); "Amazing Grace" (378); and "How Firm a Foundation" (529) were sung with emotion and enthusiasm. "Amazing Grace," in particular, expresses the process in the Christian life of moving from sorrow to repentance to assurance of salvation to the hope of eternal life.

"Amazing grace! How sweet the sound that saved a wretch like me! I once was lost, but now am found; was blind, but now I see." That was the

Methodist camp meeting

theme of the camp meeting, and thousands claimed it as the place where they gave their lives to Jesus Christ.

Methodism was a new church for a new country, and the two grew together. Camp meetings, circuit-riding preachers, societies and classes of laypeople, and committed leadership like Francis Asbury's helped make Methodism the largest church in the United States in the nineteenth century. The church spread across the country with the wagon trains—north, south, and west, out from the cities, across rivers, over mountains, into the Great Plains, all the way to the West Coast. In the process, John Wesley's message of holy living developed a distinctive American accent.

Chapter 3

Jacob Albright, Philip William Otterbein, Martin Boehm: Holy Living in a New Language

Soon Methodism acquired more than an American accent. Others heard the Methodist message in their own languages. This segment of the story is about three people who spoke German and heard God's call to preach in that language. In the process, two new churches came into being.

Jacob Albright's parents had emigrated to America from Germany. He was born in Pennsylvania, served in the Revolutionary War, got married, and settled on his own farm. In the 1790's a dysentery epidemic killed several of Albright's children. His grief and despair drove him to his knees, as he questioned God's purposes and his own faith. Friends, pastors, and prayers brought him inner peace and an experience of God's healing love.

In response, Albright began preaching the good news of God's love in the towns and villages around his home. He stressed that those who long for a closer relationship with God and forgiveness of their sins need a change of heart. Simply obeying the teachings of the church one attends is not enough. Some local preachers opposed Albright, and he was beaten up at least once. But just as with John Wesley, many heard his message; and by 1800 he had formed three small groups of people who considered themselves "Albright's People." Three years later, this growing body declared that they were a new church, and eventually took the name The Evangelical Association. They ordained Jacob Albright as their pastor, and later as their bishop.

The form of the new church was Methodist; in fact, they used German translations of Methodist publications. But they wanted to maintain their own identity, not simply blend into the larger Methodist fold. The same was true with another church, the Church of the United Brethren in Christ, founded by two preachers, Philip William Otterbein and Martin Boehm.

In 1752, at the age of twenty-five, Philip William Otterbein left his home

Martin Boehm

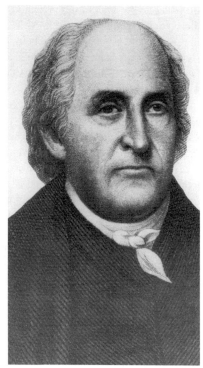

William Otterbein

in Germany to become a missionary to German settlers in Pennsylvania. He was a pastor in the German Reformed Church, and preached a message of salvation and assurance that he himself did not feel. Eventually, through prayer and spiritual struggle, he came to a realization of God's love and forgiveness, much as John Wesley had at his Aldersgate experience. Like Wesley, Otterbein's preaching stressed the "warmed heart" experience of salvation; and like Wesley, he too stressed the importance of living a holy life. He was a good friend of Francis Asbury's and participated in Asbury's ordination in 1784.

Another preacher, Martin Boehm, preached this same message of God's love and holy living. Boehm was a Mennonite from a Swiss family, and his native tongue was German. His church, following the New Testament practice, cast lots to select their preacher. Boehm was selected, but he felt completely inadequate for the task. As he struggled with his feelings, he too, like Wesley, Albright, and Otterbein, had a transforming religious experience and soon began preaching to great crowds. At one such meeting, Otterbein heard him preach. After Boehm finished, Otterbein, overcome with emotion, came forward and threw his arms around Boehm, exclaiming "Wir sind Brüder!" ("We are Brethren!") (as quoted in *The History of the Evangelical United Brethren Church,* by J. Bruce Behney and Paul H. Eller; Abingdon, 1979; page 39). Boehm and Otterbein became the leaders of a group of like-minded believers. Eventually, they organized formally as a church, the United Brethren in Christ, taking their name from Otterbein's famous words.

In 1946, these two German-speaking churches (The Evangelical Church [formed by union of The Evangelical Association and The United Evangelical Church] and the Church of the United Brethren in Christ) joined together as The Evangelical United Brethren Church. Then in 1968, they came together with the Methodists to form The United Methodist Church. So, a movement that started in the heart of one man, John Wesley, spread through England and all across America, in English, in German, and ultimately in many other languages. Along with John Wesley, we can claim Charles Wesley, Francis Asbury, Jacob Albright, Philip William Otterbein, and Martin Boehm as founders of our tradition. But our church is not simply the child of its founders, just as you are not simply a child of your parents. You have been shaped and changed by your experiences; and our church has been shaped by its responses to the needs, issues, and circumstances of the times it has lived through.

Chapter 4

Unity and Diversity

United Methodism has a strong heritage of diversity and tolerance. John Wesley himself set the tone:

"Condemn no man for not thinking as you think: Let every one enjoy the full and free liberty of thinking for himself: Let every man use his own judgment, since every man must give an account of himself to God" (from "Advice to the People Called Methodists" [October 10, 1745], in *The Works of the Rev. John Wesley,* Volume VIII; page 357).

"But as to all opinions which do not strike at the root of Christianity, we think and let think" (from "The Character of a Methodist," in *The Works of the Rev. John Wesley*, Volume VIII; page 340).

The only requirement for joining the first Methodist societies was a desire to know and follow God. Where people lived, how they voted, or how much was in their bank account didn't matter. Wesley and his preachers welcomed all who would accept God's forgiving, transforming love.

Ideally, Methodists are open and welcoming to people with differing attitudes and political positions, and to those from all countries and races. (At least that's how it works much of the time.) We United Methodists are both conservative and liberal. We're rich, poor, and in-between. We speak dozens of languages and worship in distinctive ways. Our skin colors and our cultural backgrounds are a rainbow of beautiful differences.

Achieving the goals of unity and diversity has been difficult over the years. Sometimes it's tough to call a person "sister" or "brother" when he or she holds political views you think are wrong, does things you disagree with, or has a different accent or skin color or way of dressing. Our history as a country and as United Methodists includes painful episodes of division,

Harry Hosier

anger, and injustice toward those who are somehow "different."

One of the first big challenges within Methodism was dealing with the reality of slavery. John Wesley spoke out against slavery, believing that it was an evil practice. The last letter he wrote, several days before he died, was to encourage a reformer who was working to abolish the slave trade in England.

At the time Methodism took root in the American colonies, slavery was legal throughout the country, not just in the South. Over the years, the Northern states gradually abolished slave trading. But in both the North and the South many whites believed that blacks were inferior, even sub-human. And many people had a vested financial interest in preserving the business of slavery.

Nevertheless, Methodists preached to black as well as white; and thousands of African Americans joined the Methodist movement. The first Methodist group in America, the one led by Barbara Heck and Philip Embury, included Betty, an African American who was Barbara Heck's servant. And one of Francis Asbury's closest associates was Harry Hosier, an African American. Called "Black Harry," he was a powerful, eloquent preacher, much admired by those who heard him, both black and white. Harry Hosier was born a slave and was later freed. He traveled with Asbury and other Methodist preachers. When asked how it was that he preached so eloquently, even though he was uneducated, he replied, "I sing by faith, pray by faith, preach by faith, and do everything by faith; without faith in the Lord Jesus I can do nothing" (as quoted in *Harry Hosier, Circuit Rider,* by Warren Thomas Smith; Abingdon Press, 1994; pages 24 and 25).

Despite the witness of leaders like Harry Hosier, racial tensions were evident, and division was almost inevitable. In Philadelphia, Richard Allen, an African American and a former slave, led a group of fellow members out of a predominantly white Methodist congregation after they were prevented from worshiping on an equal basis. Eventually, Allen became the first bishop of The African Methodist Episcopal Church. In a similar way, black members of a New York City church decided to form their own congregation. They became The African Methodist Episcopal Zion Church. A third African American denomination, The Christian Methodist Episcopal Church, was formed after the Civil War (until 1954, the name was The Colored Methodist Episcopal Church). All three denominations followed John Wesley's teaching, but have traveled the Methodist way independently, founding churches, missions, and schools around the world. But not all African American Methodists left to join the new denominations. Most, in fact, stayed in The Methodist Episcopal Church, witnessing to their faith and working for racial equality.

The Methodist Episcopal Church, organized in 1784, prohibited members from owning slaves. That position softened over the years as many slaveholders joined the church, but there were others who wanted the church to hold a strong anti-slavery position. In 1843, a group of Northern white Methodists, fed up with the church's unwillingness to speak out boldly against slavery, pulled out and formed their own church, the Wesleyan Methodist Connection of America (today called the Wesleyan Church). A protest against wishy-washy Methodist attitudes toward slavery also played a part in the formation of the Free Methodist Church in 1860.

The biggest controversy erupted in 1844. A Methodist bishop had inherited two slaves from his wife; and although the bishop was determined to free the slaves, the fact that he owned the slaves at all lit the match that set fire to the North/South conflict in the church. The Northern delegates voted not to allow the bishop to serve while he owned slaves. The Southern delegates refused to accept that vote, with the result that fifteen Southern annual conferences met in Louisville, Kentucky, in May 1845, and organized a new church, The Methodist Episcopal Church, South.

The Methodists were not the only ones to be affected by the slavery issue; the Presbyterian and Baptist churches also split into Northern and Southern denominations. The separation of churches into two branches was an omen of what would soon happen to the whole country during the Civil War, fifteen years later.

Just after the Civil War, some folk tried to reunite the two Methodist churches, but without success. So, for nearly a century, The Methodist Episcopal Church and The Methodist Episcopal Church, South, developed separately, each running its own schools and missions, publishing its own literature, building its own churches, and training its own preachers. Finally, in 1939, the time had come. Together with The Methodist Protestant Church, the Northern and Southern branches reunited and formed The Methodist Church.

Mary McLeod Bethune

Once the Civil War was over and slavery was ended, racial problems continued. Former slaves were not treated equally. Generations of reformers have worked together to try to create a church and a world where black and white can live together in equality and harmony. Sometimes the church has led the fight for tolerance, and sometimes it has lagged far behind. In 1939, at the time of the merger that created The Methodist Church, it made a decision that many then and now have interpreted as a step backward.

When the Northern and Southern branches of Methodism reunited in 1939, they divided the country into jurisdictions. Five geographical divisions were formed to help administer the church. The new church also decided to form a Central Jurisdiction. Rather than a geographical division, it extended all over the country and was limited to black churches. To many people, both black and white, this was a form of segregation. At the General Conference that made the decision, many voices spoke out against it.

One of the most eloquent voices was that of Mary McLeod Bethune, the daughter of slaves and a prominent educator, activist, and government official. At the 1936 General Conference when the creation of the Central Jurisdiction was being debated, she was a delegate and spoke in opposition: "I have not been able to make my mind see it clearly enough to be willing to have the history of this General Conference written, and the Negro youths of fifty or a hundred years from today read and find that Mary McLeod Bethune acquiesced to anything that looked like segregation to black people. . . . I am very sorry that I shall not be able to give my vote to the united effort that we all so much desire. What would Jesus do? Answer for yourselves" (from *The Daily Christian Advocate* [Methodist Episcopal Church], May 5, 1936; page 90). But she was outvoted, and for nearly thirty years the Central Jurisdiction was a part of The Methodist Church. It was eliminated when The United Methodist Church was formed in 1968.

Although the Central Jurisdiction has been viewed by many as a bad compromise on a sensitive issue, Methodists have been leaders in working for racial harmony and equality. Immediately after the Civil War, they founded schools to educate freed slaves, like Meharry Medical School in Nashville and Rust College in Little Rock, Arkansas. During the civil rights movement of the 1960's, Methodists marched in Selma, rallied in Washington, and lobbied Congress on civil rights causes. Most United Methodists are proud of the racial and ethnic diversity in our church, and strive toward harmony and equality for all people.

United Methodists are also persons of Hispanic, Asian, Pacific Island, and Native American heritage, illustrating that John Wesley's message of holy living crosses language and cultural boundaries. Sometimes words don't even matter. God spoke to Alejo Hernández in a language not his own. Hernández was a Mexican soldier who longed to learn about the Bible. He traveled to Brownsville, Texas, to an English-speaking Protestant worship service. He later wrote, "I was seated where I could see the congregation but few could see me. I felt that God's spirit was there, although I could not understand a word that was being said. I felt my heart strangely warmed. . . . I went away weeping for joy" (as quoted in *Each in Our Own Tongue*, edited by Justo L. González; Abingdon Press, 1991; page 42). He eventually became the first Mexican ordained by a Methodist denomination. He served as a missionary in Mexico City and planted the seed of the gospel in the short time he was there before he died in 1875 at the age of thirty-three.

Our diversity has extended to European ethnic groups, as well. From the

German-speaking Methodist groups like The Evangelical Association and the United Brethren to Swedish, Italian, French, or Bulgarian, immigrants to this country have been drawn to the family of John Wesley's followers. And Methodism has gone to other countries as well. The result is a worldwide church, with many different ways to worship. As United Methodists, our cultural differences enrich us. Every person of every ethnic heritage adds color and flavor and texture to the unique mix that is United Methodism.

And then there are less obvious differences among United Methodists. Not skin color or cultural heritage or vocal accent, but political beliefs and social attitudes. We have seen how differing opinions about slavery tore the church apart in the nineteenth century. Today's issues are different, but can threaten our unity just as much. Abortion, homosexuality, school prayer, welfare reform, gun control—in almost any United Methodist congregation, you will find people on all sides of the hottest topics of the day. Can we worship together in harmony even when we disagree on important issues? Can we celebrate both unity and diversity?

Wanting to be around those who look like us or who share our opinions and ideas is a natural impulse. But that's not how God made the world. God made every person unique and irreplaceable, and each has his or her unique ideas and beliefs. God also gave us the church, a place where we come together in a community to worship and work.

However, we don't have to pretend that important issues don't matter to us, or that we don't feel strongly about something. Disagreements need not be disastrous; in fact, the church should be the best place for discussions on sensitive issues, because it should be the place where people know they are loved and accepted as children of God.

Actively loving those who are different from us is part of who we are as The United Methodist Church. Sometimes the lesson is a hard one, because it goes against everything the world teaches; but we keep on learning. We keep trying to live up to John Wesley's opinion of Methodists:

"It is the glory of the people called Methodists that they condemn none for their opinions or modes of worship. They think and let think, and insist upon nothing but faith working by love" (from Letter to Mrs. Howton, October 3, 1783, in *The Letters of the Rev. John Wesley,* Volume VII, edited by John Telford; London: The Epworth Press, 1931; page 190).

Chapter 5

Where Do Women Belong?

I magine a world where your mother couldn't vote; where your grandmother couldn't own a home; where your aunt couldn't open a bank account by herself. Imagine a church where women couldn't preach or serve Holy Communion. Does that seem strange to you? In fact, it wasn't so long ago that the world of women was a restricted place, both in the church and in American society. Women fought for decades for the right to vote, finally

Marjorie Matthews

winning victory in 1920 with the Nineteenth Amendment. Women also fought for the right to hold leadership positions in the church, especially as ordained clergy. They won small victories all along the way, but it wasn't until 1956 that Methodist women could be fully ordained. For Evangelical and United Brethren women, final victory came in 1968 (the United Brethren General Conference of 1889 had approved ordination of women, but the practice was not widespread). When Marjorie Matthews was elected the first woman bishop in 1980, many people felt that it was the dawn of a new age of women's participation in the church.

What would John Wesley think

of our church, with its women clergy and women bishops? No doubt it would be a real adjustment for him, because his world was different. But Wesley knew that the Holy Spirit calls both women and men to serve God in many ways, and Wesley was never one to stand in the way of the Spirit. He also was not afraid to try new things or to change his mind, although sometimes it took a little persuading.

Wesley learned two things early in his ministry: The first was that his renewal movement would thrive only if laypeople, the members of the Methodist societies, were committed to its success. Many of those laypeople were women. John Wesley even gave some of those women leadership positions in his movement, which was unusual for the eighteenth century.

Mary Bosanquet Fletcher

The second thing Wesley learned was that laypeople, both women and men, could be called by God to special tasks, like preaching. In those days only ordained clergy preached. Like many people of his day, Wesley concurred with this situation; the thought of a layperson preaching was hard for him to swallow. His mother, Susanna Wesley, was the person who influenced him on that issue. When a layman, Thomas Maxfield, preached at the Methodist headquarters in London in Wesley's absence, Wesley was upset at first. It just wasn't proper for a layperson to fill a role meant for ordained clergy. But Susanna, who had heard Maxfield preach, set her son straight, telling him that Maxfield "is as truly called of God to preach as you are. Examine what have been the fruits of his preaching and hear him yourself" (as quoted in *Reasonable Enthusiast: John Wesley and the Rise of Methodism*; page 210).

Wesley had enough flexibility to see the wisdom of his mother's words, and he began opening the door for laypeople to preach in Methodist meetings. Soon it became obvious that lay preaching was one of the most important tools in the spread of Methodism. Wesley became so convinced of its importance that he defied all criticism from the Church of England (to which most Methodists belonged before the formation of a separate church). He once wrote, "Therefore, if we cannot stop a separation [from the Church of England] without stopping lay-Preachers, the case is clear,—we cannot stop it at all" (from A Letter to the Reverend Mr. Walker [September 24, 1755], in *The Works of the Rev. John Wesley*, Volume XIII; page 196).

Wesley, then, was able to go from opposing lay preaching to defying his own church to support it. What does that have to do with women? Well, many laypeople were women; and some of them felt called of God to preach. This was something that the culture, both in and out of the church, did not readily accept. A woman's place was at home, behind the scenes, not up in front of others (meaning men) telling them what to do.

Wesley was not out to make huge changes in how his culture viewed women; but he knew, above all, that God works in human hearts. Even if the world disapproves, it is more important than anything else to follow God's leading. When one of his most active followers, Mary Bosanquet, wrote to Wesley telling him that she had heard God's call to preach, he responded [with a letter dated June 13, 1771] that it was clear that she had an "*extraordinary* call" to preach. He continued, . . ."the whole work of God termed Methodism is an extraordinary dispensation of His providence. Therefore I do not wonder if several things occur therein which do not fall under the ordinary rules of discipline" (*The Letters of the Rev. John Wesley*, Volume V; page 257).

If John Wesley ever wondered about women's spiritual leadership, he only had to look at the life and example of his own mother. Susanna Wesley didn't preach, but she was a spiritual leader in her own way. Once, when her husband was away, Susanna wasn't at all satisfied with the substitute preacher. Not only were his sermons weak, but he also made insulting remarks about her husband from the pulpit. Concerned about the lack of spiritual nourishment for her children and the family's servants, Susanna began holding services in her kitchen on Sunday evenings. She led the group in singing psalms, and read prayers and sermons from the family library. The services were originally intended just for the Wesley family circle, but the servants invited their families and friends and the crowd grew larger each week. Samuel, off in London, heard about it and wrote her a letter telling her to stop.

Susanna responded with her own letter [dated February 6, 1711-12], defending what she had done as obedience to God. She said, "In your absence, I cannot but look upon every soul you leave under my care, as a talent committed to me under a trust, by the great Lord of all the families, both of heaven and earth. And if I am unfaithful to him or you, in neglecting to improve these talents, how shall I answer

Susanna Wesley

unto him, when he shall command me to render an account of my stewardship?" (from *The Works of the Rev. John Wesley,* Volume I; Wesleyan-Methodist Book-Room, 1872; page 385). Susanna continued the services. John Wesley learned early that God could and did work through women.

As Methodism spread across America, women's contributions kept the churches in their communities growing and active. The question of women's role in the church grew, too. Should women preach? Should they be ordained, set apart in a special way to serve God and the church? The debate went on for decades. The Evangelical Association never did approve ordination for women. The United Brethren and the Methodist branches eventually did ordain women, although sometimes they didn't grant them the same rights and authority as men. The pioneers were those women who

Anna Oliver

decided that, no matter what, they would follow God's call.

One such woman was Anna Oliver. Her full name was actually Vivianna Olivia Snowden; but when she heard God's call to the ordained ministry, she changed her name so she wouldn't embarrass her family. She contacted dozens of seminaries, asking to be enrolled as a full-time student. Only one, the Methodist seminary in Boston, agreed to her request. After several years of struggle, hard work, and opposition, Anna Oliver graduated in 1876, the first woman in America to earn a full-fledged seminary degree. Although her denomination refused to ordain her, she served the church as a pastor in New Jersey and in Brooklyn, New York, for the rest of her life.

Here is how Anna described the personal consequences of answering God's call: "I have made almost every conceivable sacrifice to do what I believe God's will. . . . I gave up home, friends and support, . . . worked for several years to constant exhaustion, and suffered cold, hunger, and loneliness. The things hardest for me to bear were laid upon me. For two months my own mother did not speak to me. When I entered the house she turned and walked away. . . . However, I take no credit to myself for enduring these trials, because at every step it was plain to me, that I had no alternative but to go forward or renounce my Lord." Pioneers like Anna Oliver paved the way for women to become ordained pastors and, eventually, bishops of The United Methodist Church.

And what about women who didn't necessarily seek ordination, but simply wanted a greater voice in the church? The whole question of the rights of laypeople plagued Methodism from the start. The early Methodist movement was clergy-oriented. Ordained pastors made the decisions about the church's ministry and mission. Laymen and laywomen were shut out of the process. Laity rights was one of the earliest battlegrounds in American Methodism, and the cause of one of its earliest divisions. During the late 1820's, a number of clergy and laity became increasingly unhappy with the policies of The Methodist Episcopal Church. These differences led to the official formation of The Methodist Protestant Church in 1830. This new branch of Methodism did not elect bishops, and it gave laity a greater voice in church government. Methodist Protestants were also more receptive to women's leadership, both as laity and as ordained clergy.

In 1892, when the Methodist Protestant General Conference debated whether to allow women delegates, one of the proposed delegates, the Reverend Eugenia St. John (she had been ordained three years earlier), spoke to the [male] delegates: "There is a serious question now before you . . . . Dare this conference stand before the omen given by God and frustrate his will for the upbuilding of your church by your prejudices? . . . The great question of the future is whether you will have power to conquer the forces of sin, and I tell you it will need every woman that can be found to stand side by side with the good-minded men in this work if the church is to be triumphant" (as quoted in *Methodist Recorder*, June 4, 1892). After listening to a speech like that, it shouldn't be any surprise that the delegates voted to let women join their ranks.

Over the next thirty years, the other denominations fought the battle for laity rights. The United Brethren were next to give women voting rights, and the Northern and Southern branches of The Methodist Episcopal Church eventually followed suit. The Evangelical Association, though, never ordained women; nor did it grant them laity rights.

In 1939, the Methodist Protestants came together with The Methodist Episcopal Church and The Methodist Episcopal Church, South, to form The Methodist Church. By that time, Methodists were beginning to understand that the answer to the question, "Where do women belong?" is "anywhere that God calls them to serve."

Chapter 6

Go Into All the World

Here's a challenge: Locate a country in the world where no church claims John Wesley as its ancestor. From England to China, Belgium to the Fiji Islands, you can worship with Methodists and their cousins of the Wesleyan tradition. Methodists have grown from a small renewal movement in England to a worldwide fellowship of Wesley's children. For almost three hundred years, Methodists have taken seriously Jesus' call to go into all the world and preach the good news. John Wesley phrased it this way: "I look upon the whole world as my parish."

From England, John Wesley's preachers traveled to Wales, Ireland, and the Americas. Wesley assigned Thomas Coke, often called the father of Methodist missions, to oversee the work in America along with Francis Asbury. Coke believed passionately in the spread of the gospel to every land. He worked for years to bring Methodism to the Caribbean, Africa,

John Stewart preaching to the Wyandott Indians

India, and Ceylon. In fact, he died at sea in 1814, traveling to establish a new mission in Ceylon.

In the United States, the missions movement began with John Stewart. We know he was of mixed parentage, possibly part African American and part Native American, which meant that he faced a lot of prejudice. As a young man John Stewart lived a wild life. He drank too much, got into fights, didn't stick with any job, and drifted from place to place. Finally, he sank so low that the only way out was up. That was when he committed his life to Christ and began to follow the Wesleyan way of holy living.

One day, John Stewart went into the fields to pray; and, as he later reported, "It seemed to me . . . that I heard a voice, like the voice of a woman praising God; and then another, as the voice of a man, saying to me, 'You must declare my counsel faithfully.'. . . They seemed to come from a northwest direction" (as quoted in *History of the Wyandott Mission*, by James B. Finley; Cincinnati: The Book Concern, 1840; page 76). Stewart immediately packed his knapsack and set off in the direction of the voices. Eventually he arrived at a settlement of the Wyandott tribe in Ohio. He settled among the Wyandott, and his preaching and beautiful singing voice drew many hearers. Word soon spread of his success; and within a few years, Methodist preachers were so convinced of the importance of his work that they formed an organization to support it.

That organization, begun in 1819, was the Missionary Society of The Methodist Episcopal Church. The work with the Wyandott Indians was the Society's first mission; but the work soon spread to other Native American tribes, to new settlements in the American West, and to most of the countries of the world. Other branches of the United Methodist family tree soon formed their own missionary societies; and by the 1870's, one could find Methodist, Evangelical, and United Brethren missionaries all over the world.

For many missionaries, speaking the gospel in an unfamiliar language with people from a different culture called for tremendous commitment. Physical conditions could be unhealthy or fatal in the days before modern medicines. In some cultures, active hostility to the Christian message endangered missionaries' lives and property. Yet hundreds answered God's call to minister to the spiritual and physical needs of God's children everywhere. They organized schools, established hospitals, built churches, and ran orphanages. They preached, prayed, taught, and sang. They trained native-born Christians to share the gospel themselves. Above all, in their lives they tried to practice holy living.

There are still those who answer God's call. What started as a small missionary society in 1819 is now the General Board of Global Ministries of The United Methodist Church. That board still sends missionaries all over the world, still supports schools, hospitals, and hundreds of projects to make people's lives better. Truly, the whole world is our parish.

For United Methodists, missions involves any situation where people are in need; and those situations are often in our own back yard. Maybe it's a church-sponsored literacy project in the slums of Chicago or a new church for a rural community in Oklahoma. Some of our "back-yard missions" have a long history. In the mountains of Kentucky, for example, a mission began in 1921 that today is still a vital part of The United Methodist Church.

Southeastern Kentucky is a wild and beautiful area of mountains, rivers, and isolated towns in the heart of Appalachia. It is also an area where life can be hard and where economic conditions are poor. In 1921, there weren't many churches there; but there were faithful Christians who prayed for God to send preachers and teachers who could lead the people.

The Evangelical Association (the spiritual descendants of Jacob Albright) answered the call. In December 1920, the secretary of the missionary society and a church bishop went to the Red Bird area (named for a local river) at the invitation of a local family who wanted the church to come to Red Bird. The roads were so bad in that mountainous area that it took them thirteen hours to travel twenty miles! The poverty and illness they saw on their short visit convinced them that the missionary society should begin work there as soon as possible.

The first task was to raise money to support a mission to Red Bird. The women of the denomination took on the challenge and within a few months had raised enough money to start the mission. On July 1, 1921, the first workers, two women, arrived at the town of Beverly. They were teachers, and their first task was to start teaching in the badly understaffed public schools. They also immediately organized Sunday schools.

Soon Rev. John J. DeWall arrived with his family to take charge of the work. On January 29, 1922, more than 150 people attended the dedication of a new building designed to serve both as a church and a school. Over the next few years the work spread into the small communities around Beverly.

The missionaries became part of the fabric of those little towns. Like every-body else in the area, the missionaries walked the mountain trails from house to house. They waited for weeks for supplies to come over the mountains. They learned firsthand about how hard, and how beautiful, life could be in Appalachia.

The missionaries also witnessed the joy that new life in Christ brings to those who were once in despair. They saw that hungry people were fed. The mission soon opened two schools that enrolled over two hundred children and young people who otherwise might not have received any education at all. Through the missionaries and the dedicated Christians of Red Bird, sick people and older adults received pastoral care and medical attention.

Lydia B. Rice, a registered nurse, came to Red Bird in the summer of 1922; and for four years she was the only medical worker at the mission. She traveled like the early Methodist preachers, on her horse, Major. She rode along the narrow mountain trails from house to house, carrying medicine in her saddlebags. One of the first things she found was that typhoid fever was a common disease in the area, even though there was a vaccine that had virtually eliminated it in other parts of the country. Lydia Rice brought the vaccine to Red Bird and saved countless lives.

Because so many people lived in poverty, she spent a lot of time teaching basic sanitation and health care to children at school and adults at home. The mission set up a hospital in the girls' dormitory at the Beverly school; and until other medical missionaries joined her, Miss Rice was totally responsible for the patients' care. Because of the missionaries' commitment, and the support of faithful church members, the Red Bird Mission thrived.

The missionaries couldn't solve every problem, of course. Today, the Red Bird Missionary Conference of The United Methodist Church still battles poverty, alcohol and drug abuse, despair, loneliness, and illness. But the church and its outreach remain a strong Christian presence in the Cumberland Mountains of eastern Kentucky. Missionaries teach, preach, give medical care, and provide connection and hope for people who feel isolated and hopeless. Even more importantly, the churches of the Red Bird Conference are filled with those who celebrate Christ's presence in their lives and seek to bring others to know him. The work begun in 1921 continues.

Women have always played a leading role in missions in the United Methodist tradition. Some have stayed home to raise support while others have served on the mission field as teachers, doctors, evangelists, or administrators. The first American Methodist women to serve as missionaries went to Liberia in the 1830's. Liberia was established on the West African coast as a home for freed American slaves. Many of those former slaves were Methodists, and they wanted pastors to come and minister to them in their new home. The Missionary Society sent the first missionaries to Liberia to care for the settlers and, hopefully, to bring the gospel to millions of native Africans in the continent's interior.

One of those first missionaries was a woman named Sophronia Farrington. She sailed to Liberia in 1833 with two married couples. Soon after they arrived in Liberia, all five became ill with malaria. One of the wives died, and her husband and the other couple decided they had to return to America to save their lives. Sophronia Farrington was also ill, but she refused to go. In a letter home, she wrote, "The doctor has said it was not possible for my constitution to endure the climate, and advised the missionaries to send me home. . . . But I have absolutely refused to go. . . . I laid my life on the altar on leaving America, and I am willing that it should remain there. The hand which led me to New England, and from there here, will sever the silver cord at the most proper time; and till then death can have no power" (as quoted in *The African Repository and Colonial Journal,* Volume 10, Number 4, June 1834; pages 122–123).

Sophronia Farrington and other pioneer women missionaries inspired a whole generation of women who supported the mission work of the Methodist, Evangelical, and United Brethren churches. By the time of Sophronia Farrington's death in 1880, women's missionary societies were raising hundreds of thousands of dollars to support hospitals, schools, and a wide range of ministries all over the world.

Sometimes "mission" is in your own back yard, and sometimes it's halfway across the world. Wherever missionaries go, they try to bring God's love to people in need. When people respond to the message of salvation in Christ, they take responsibility for the church and its ministries themselves, whether they are in China, Africa, or rural America. In Korea, the life of one woman illustrates how the whole process works.

Helen Kim was born in 1899 and was given the name Kideuk Kim. When Kideuk was a small child, her mother made friends with a woman named Helen Kim, who was no relation to the family. Helen Kim was a

Bible woman, a Christian convert who worked with the missionaries bringing the gospel to people in her neighborhood. Through her influence, both of Kideuk's parents became Christians. The entire family was baptized; and Kideuk's mother and the younger children were given new names, representing their new lives. Kideuk's Korean name was changed to Whallan, and she was also given the Western name of Helen.

When Helen was sixteen, she responded to God's call to a deeper personal relationship with Jesus Christ. After experiencing God's forgiveness, she had a vision that directed her to dedicate her life to the betterment of the women of Korea. "[God] pointed out to me a big dug-out moat where a mass of Korean women were crying out for help with their hands out-

Helen Kim

stretched from the haze and confusion that covered them. The whole vision was very real to me.... From that time on, my life has been directed by God's hand toward the one course of humble service to the womanhood of my country and the emancipation of the women of the world" (from *Grace Sufficient: The Story of Helen Kim*, by herself; The Upper Room, 1964; page 30).

Most Korean girls received no education, but Helen's parents wanted her to go to school. When she was eight, they enrolled her in Ewha Haktang, a school for girls that was run by Methodist missionaries. A missionary named Mary F. Scranton had started the school in her home thirteen years before Helen Kim was born.

Later, Helen attended Ewha College. Right after graduation, she became a teacher at the school. She believed that through teaching

Korea's young women she could reach those outstretched hands in her vision. Early on, she realized that she needed more education. She came to the United Sates and eventually earned a Ph.D, the first Korean woman to achieve that level of education.

After returning to Korea, she continued teaching, then became the dean, and then the president of the school. She was the first Korean president; all the others had been missionaries. She stepped into the position because of a difficult situation. Japan had invaded and occupied Korea, and in 1940 the American missionaries were forced to leave the country.

The next year, Japan and the United States entered World War II as enemies. Since Ewha College had been founded and run by American missionaries, the Japanese occupation forces were suspicious of anyone associated with the school. All Christian teaching was suspect as well, which made things harder for Helen Kim and the Ewha College faculty.

But Ehwa survived World War II. In 1945 it became a university, with nine hundred students. In 1948, Korea was divided into two countries. In 1950, North Korean soldiers attacked South Korea; and for the next few years, Helen Kim again faced danger in the midst of war. This time the battles were fought dangerously close to home. She had to flee her school and her home for three years.

When Helen Kim was allowed to return to Ewha, many school buildings had been damaged during the war. But classes soon opened and repairs were made. Helen Kim remained president of Ewha University from 1945 until her retirement in 1961. She also became a leader in the Methodist denomination and a strong proponent of Korean culture and of the right of women everywhere to be liberated and educated. She represented Korea in the United Nations and on other international bodies. By the time of her retirement, Ewha had eight thousand students. Today it has over nineteen thousand students and is the largest school for women in the world.

Similar stories can be told from all over the world. Missionaries still bring hope and healing to the world. In the former Soviet Union, Methodists are working along with the Orthodox Church and other Christian denominations to bring the gospel to people who are now worshiping freely once again. And on the African continent, Africa University is a symbol of United Methodism's commitment to God's people everywhere.

Back in 1898, Methodist bishop Joseph Crane Hartzell opened a mission

Ewha University

at Old Mutare, Zimbabwe, and dreamed of young people coming to this site from all directions, speaking many languages. That dream is coming true now, as students from all over the continent of Africa come to attend the new university, opened in 1992. Africa University is the first United Methodist-related university on the African continent.

Thousands of United Methodists have shared Bishop Hartzell's dream and have given of their money, their time, and their skills to make the dream come true. Some have sent money; others have donated books to the university library. Teams from churches all over the United States have traveled to Zimbabwe to construct buildings and roads. Because of the university, gifted students no longer have to travel to America or Europe to receive seminary training and advanced degrees in other subjects. The university is training the future leaders of African society and of The United Methodist Church.

From the voices calling a young man to preach to the Wyandotts in Ohio all the way to the voices of the students at Africa University, the story of The United Methodist Church is one of a mission-minded people. Wouldn't John Stewart be amazed!

Chapter 7

Making the World a Better Place

United Methodists are known for working to make the world a better place, by helping the helpless, confronting evil, and putting our faith into action. Instead of throwing our hands up in despair, we put our hands to work helping other people.

The United Methodist heritage of social action goes back to John and Charles Wesley's years at Oxford University. The brothers and their circle of friends responded with Christian love to the needs they saw around them. They visited prisoners, many of whom were had been jailed because they couldn't pay their bills. They collected food, clothing, and medicine for poor people and visited in their homes.

Other students ridiculed the Wesleys and their friends for their efforts, sarcastically calling them "the Holy Club" and "the Godly Club"; but the Wesleys were convinced that they must put their faith into action. John Wesley reminded his critics that Jesus told his followers that when we help others, it is just like helping Jesus himself.

The Holy Club

Richard Allen

As Wesley and his followers began preaching and organizing all over England, they told people that being a Christian meant *doing* good, not just *being* good. Holy living meant *living* one's faith. Methodists continued and expanded on the Holy Club's activities, offering physical care as well as spiritual comfort to the poor, the sick, the needy, and the imprisoned. Wesley's societies lent money to small businesses. Medicines were available at Methodist preaching houses, to be dispensed to the needy. Methodists opened schools, homes for older adults, and orphanages. Being a Wesleyan Christian was a full-time job.

Methodists in the United States had that same kind of energy and commitment. Some were willing to risk their lives to help others. In 1793, a yellow fever epidemic invaded the city of Philadelphia. A person infected with yellow fever became ill quickly, and could die just as quickly. When the epidemic struck Philadelphia, healthy people fled the city in terror. Sick people were left without help, and there was no one to bury the dead.

Do you remember Richard Allen, an African American Methodist who left the predominantly white church to form the African Methodist Episcopal Church? During the yellow fever epidemic, Allen's congregation stayed in the city, ministering to the sick, burying the dead, and risking their own lives. They lived out their faith in the most dangerous, desperate circumstances, sure that this was what God had called them to do. Richard Allen later wrote, "The Lord was pleased to strengthen us and remove all fear from us, and disposed our hearts to be as useful as possible."

The courage of those who face down an epidemic is clear. There is also another kind of courage, one that involves fighting what you think is wrong even when people disagree with you.

For instance, from the beginning, Methodists spoke out against alcohol abuse. One of John Wesley's rules for people who wanted to join the Methodist societies was that they must avoid "drunkenness, *buying or selling spirituous liquors*; or *drinking them* (unless in cases of extreme necessity)" [when alcohol is used as a medicine]. Methodists were to be temperate, or moderate, in their use of alcohol; the word *temperance* was used to describe their position.

In December 1873, in Hillsboro, Ohio, a group of women began a crusade against alcohol. Their most public tactic was to gather in small groups in front of saloons and kneel in prayer. Soon, women in hundreds

Frances Willard

of towns and cities were doing the same thing. These women had no idea that they were launching a worldwide movement, but that's what happened. Within a year the Woman's Christian Temperance Union was systematically fighting alcohol abuse. The women came together out of a shared concern for the effects of alcohol abuse on women, children, and families.

How could women fight this battle? In those days they had no political power. They couldn't even vote! The Temperance Union needed strong leadership that could transform concerned women into a political and social force to be reckoned with. Frances Willard was that leader. She was a Methodist laywoman; and by the end of her life, she was one of the most famous American women.

Frances grew up on a farm in Wisconsin. She idolized her older brother and wanted to do whatever he did. When he went off to cast his first vote in an election, she knew that this was one thing she couldn't do just like him, since women couldn't vote. The memory of that injustice stayed with her for the rest of her life.

Frances went to college and became a teacher, but it wasn't a satisfying career for her. At the age of thirty-five, she found her true calling, as an organizer, administrator, lecturer, and inspiration to thousands of women. Frances joined the Temperance Union and soon became its president, a position she held for nearly the rest of her life. Her slogan for the Union was "Do Everything," and she lived by that slogan. For her, temperance was just one part of a wide-ranging social reform agenda.

Frances was active in prison reform, especially as it concerned women prisoners. She worked to strengthen laws against rape. She worked for better education for the poor, better sanitation in overcrowded cities, and was a strong supporter of the labor movement, particularly as it concerned the rights of women and children. Most of all, she wanted women to be able to vote. For social reform to work, it had to be supported by the force of law. Factory owners, for example, used children as workers because they were cheap labor. Children as young as five years old spent fourteen hours a day in deplorable conditions, working six days a week for a few pennies. Frances Willard knew that the only way to stop the practice would be to make it illegal; and she wanted women to be able to vote on that issue and many more involving the health and welfare of children, women, and families.

Frances was a popular speaker, and one of her favorite themes was the equality of women and men. In one speech she said, "Of all the fallacies ever concocted, none is more idiotic than the one indicated in the saying, 'A woman's strength consists in her weakness. . . .' Let us insist first, last, and always that gentleness is never so attractive as when joined with strength, purity never so invincible as when leagued with intelligence, beauty never so charming as when it is seen to be the embellishment of reason and the concomitant of character. What we need to sound in the ears of girlhood is *to be brave*, and in the ears of boyhood *to be gentle*. There are not two sets of virtues; and there is but one greatness of character; it is that of him (or her) who combines the noblest traits of man and woman in nature, words, and deeds" (from an address before the Woman's Christian Temperance Union at the World's Columbian Exposition in Chicago, October 16–21, 1893).

Lucy Rider Meyer

Just as John Wesley had taught, Frances Willard believed that it was her Christian duty to make the world a better place. As a young woman she had wanted to be a preacher, but she knew that her church would not ordain her. She was one of five laywomen in 1888 who were elected delegates to the General Conference of The Methodist Episcopal Church. This was a test to see whether the General Conference would allow women to be lay delegates. They did not succeed that year, but her Methodist commitment never wavered.

The world of the late nineteenth century was changing quickly. Since the Civil War, thousands of immigrants had come to America seeking a better life. They flooded already overcrowded cities, which couldn't cope with so many poor people needing homes, jobs, food, and medical care. Many factories produced too much pollution, and many factory owners treated their workers like slaves. As in John Wesley's day, it was tempting to feel overwhelmed by the needs. But, just as John Wesley had, Methodists found new ways to live their faith in a hurting world.

In 1887, a group of young Methodist women and their teacher, Lucy Rider Meyer, decided to live in Chicago over the summer to help people who lived in poor neighborhoods. Most of the people were immigrants trying to make a home for themselves in a strange country. They needed help getting jobs, learning English, and educating their children.

Soon the church officially recognized the Methodist women's work, calling the workers deaconesses. They wore plain black dresses and bonnets tied with white bows. With the distinctive attire, the deaconesses were easy to recognize in the neighborhood and didn't have to spend a lot of money on clothes.

As the deaconess movement spread, women who didn't live in the inner city ran hospitals or schools. Some deaconesses worked in rural areas; others went overseas. Today's deaconesses don't wear black dresses and bonnets anymore, but their dedication hasn't changed.

How do we make the world a better place? One way to is to share God's love with people one on one, like the deaconesses. When you give a blanket to someone who's cold, when you pray with someone who is grieving, you are showing God's love in a personal way. That kind of ministry changes lives; and when lives change, the world becomes a better place.

Another way to make the world a better place is to work for reform on a larger scale. When you write a letter to Congress to support a piece of legislation, or participate in a rally for a cause you care about, you are following in the footsteps of many United Methodist ancestors. We have already seen how Frances Willard worked to reform society through the Woman's Christian Temperance Union. She believed that institutions (such as business and government) need to get their priorities straight if people's lives are ever going to improve.

In 1907 a group of concerned Methodists organized the Methodist Federation for Social Service. (Today this agency is called the Methodist Federation for Social Action.) The organizers reminded the church that Jesus healed and helped those who were sick, or impoverished, or oppressed, as an expression of love and compassion. They also reminded the church that John Wesley urged believers to address society's ills as well as practice works of devotion.

One of the first things the Federation did was to write a Social Creed, which The Methodist Episcopal Church adopted at its 1908 General Conference. Here's what the creed said:

"The Methodist Episcopal Church stands:
For equal rights and complete justice for all men in all stations of life.
For the principle of conciliation and arbitration in industrial dissensions.
For the protection of the worker from dangerous machinery, occupational diseases, injuries, and mortality.
For the abolition of child labor.
For such regulation of the conditions of labor for women as shall safeguard the physical and moral health of the community.

44

For the suppression of the 'sweating system.'

For the gradual and reasonable reduction of the hours of labor to the lowest practical point, with work for all; and for that degree of leisure for all which is the condition of the highest human life.

For a release [from] employment one day in seven.

For a living wage in every industry.

For the highest wage that each industry can afford, and for the most equitable division of the products of industry that can ultimately be devised.

For the recognition of the Golden Rule and the mind of Christ as the supreme law of society and the sure remedy for all social ills."

As this declaration reveals, working conditions were a big social issue in 1908. While the workplace has seen many improvements over the last century, the Social Creed is still a relevant document. At General Conference every four years, the church has the chance to update the creed; and the language has been revised to reflect changing times. The Social Creed continues to express The United Methodist Church's views on social issues and social reform.

Soon after The Methodist Episcopal Church accepted the Social Creed in 1908, other denominations and church organizations endorsed it. However, some believed that the creed, and the reformers who supported it, focused too much on saving society and too little on saving souls. They felt that it was more important to focus on the spiritual needs of the individual than on economic injustice or other social problems. So at the same time that society's needs drew some people into social activism, other people were drawn to revival meetings that focused on bringing people to a saving knowledge of Jesus Christ, one by one.

The revival meetings were updated versions of the camp meeting, with lively preaching, robust singing, and an emphasis on conversion. The revivalists preached sermons designed to encourage people to realize their need for salvation and a personal relationship with Jesus Christ.

The meetings were filled with music. Many hymns in our current hymnal were written during the heyday of the revival meeting. For example, "Softy and Tenderly Jesus Is Calling" (*The United Methodist Hymnal*, 348) was often sung during revival meetings. Imagine two thousand men, women, and children, on a hot summer evening under a big tent, sitting on hard wooden benches. As the hymn is sung, dozens walk down the aisles to the altar where they kneel and pray, sometimes weeping. Over and over the hymn is sung, as dozens more come to join them, responding to the words of the hymn, "Why should we tarry when Jesus is pleading, pleading for you and for me? Why should we linger and heed not his mercies, mercies for you and for me? Come home, come home; you who are weary, come home; earnestly, tenderly, Jesus is calling, calling, O sinner, come home!"

In big cities, small towns, and country villages all over the country, revivalists urged listeners to "come home" to Jesus.

Should the church focus on winning souls for Christ, or on reforming society? Many people take the middle road and think both are important. We are called to be witnesses to God's truth, love, and justice wherever we are, in the tradition of our founders, who believed that Christians should care about people's souls—and bodies.

When we talk about making the world a better place these days, it can be hard to agree on what needs to be done. Abortion. Gay rights. Gun control. Environmental protection. You will find United Methodists on all sides of almost every issue. That's part of the diversity that makes us unique.

Despite our differences, United Methodists have a heritage of meeting needs where they find them, of speaking out on issues that concern the physical and spiritual well-being of people, and of working to improve the lives of people. Our differences shouldn't keep us from doing God's work in the world or from standing together in love. As Christians and as United Methodists, we should pay attention to John Wesley's words, "Though we can't think alike, may we not love alike? May we not be of one heart, though we are not of one opinion?" (from Sermon 39, "Catholic Spirit" [1750], in *The Works of John Wesley* [Bicentennial Edition], Volume 2; Abingdon Press, 1985; page 82).

Where does the church stand on issues like abortion rights or gun control? For the official church position on social issues, look at the Social Principles statement in our *Book of Discipline*. These items are voted on by the General Conference, which is the congress of The United Methodist Church. This body is made up of lay and clergy delegates from all over the world and meets every four years to determine the church's budget, set priorities for its missions and ministries, and clarify its positions on social, economic, and political issues.

Chapter 8

Working With Other Christians

United Methodists also join with other churches to make the world a better place. John Wesley established our historic tolerance for people who understand the Christian faith a little differently than we do: "But as to all opinions which do not strike at the root of Christianity we 'think and let think'" (from "The Character of a Methodist" [1742], in *The Works of John Wesley* [Bicentennial Edition], Volume 9; Abingdon Press, 1989; page 34).

That doesn't mean we have always been models of tolerance and understanding. Even John Wesley was pretty hard on the Roman Catholics of his time. In this country, early Methodist preachers could be quick to criticize Baptists, Presbyterians, or anyone else for their theology, their worship, or the way they got their converts.

But over the decades we have learned to come together. We have learned, and are still learning, how to "think and let think." Within our own family, we have brought together several denominations to form the present-day United Methodist Church. Within the worldwide Methodist community, we participate in the World Methodist Council, which has sixty-four member denominations that claim a connection to John Wesley's teachings. That's about twenty-five million members all over the world.

United Methodists have also been leaders in the National Council of Churches of Christ (NCC) in the U.S.A. and in the World Council of Churches (WCC). The NCC members are Christian denominations in the United States. The NCC operates ministries around the world, emphasizing education, evangelism, health care, and crisis relief. You may be familiar with one of its most well-known activities: The NCC sponsored the translations of the Bible that we call the Revised Standard Version and the New Revised Standard Version.

John R. Mott

The World Council of Churches is made up of Christian denominations across the globe. The Council has more than three hundred member churches; and, like the NCC, it helps them work together cooperatively to spread the gospel of Christ in word and deed all over the world. One of its most important programs encourages dialogue between different faith groups that are often in conflict. Protestants and Catholics, Jews and Muslims, Hindus and Buddhists have learned to talk to one another with the help of the WCC. Like the NCC, the WCC is active around the world in providing food, clothing, training, and development assistance for the poor and suffering in developing countries and in areas of natural or human disasters.

Two of the best-known leaders in ecumenical work have been members of the United Methodist family. John R. Mott was born in 1865 and grew up in Iowa. He went to college at Cornell University in New York state, and while there had a life-changing experience of God's love. That summer he pledged himself to the Student Volunteer Movement, which sent hundreds of missionaries into the world for Christ. While never a missionary in the formal sense, John Mott devoted his life to the Young Men's Christian Association (YMCA), which sought to equip laypeople for service in mission fields.

Mott saw Christ's church as a world church. He encouraged people in dozens of countries to work together in cooperative Christian organizations.

Harry Denman, like John R. Mott, was a layperson. When he died in 1976, he left no living relatives, no closet full of clothes, no home. He gave

Harry Denman

it all away for the Lord. Throughout his career with the Methodist Board of Evangelism, he traveled with two small suitcases. One held a change of clothes and the other his correspondence. That was all he ever carried, even on long trips. And did he travel! He carried the good news of Jesus Christ all over the world, speaking in dozens of foreign countries and, more important, talking one-on-one with every person he met about the love of God.

And love was Denman's watchword—a love that gives, that sacrifices, that truly cares for the other person, that transcends all distinctions of denomination. He said, "One of the things about being a Christian is that we can disagree with people without being disagreeable. . . . I cannot make people believe what I believe; all I can do is to tell them what I believe, and if I want my statement to be persuasive, then I must live it. This is what Jesus did; he lived it" (from *Prophetic Evangelist: The Living Legacy of Harry Denman*; The Upper Room, Discipleship Resources, the General Board of Discipleship, and the Foundation for Evangelism, 1993; pages 20–21).

Harry Denman and John Mott lived their faith. So did Frances Willard, Helen Kim, and Harry Hosier. All the people we have met here are part of our heritage, part of our family tree. And that tree will continue to grow, as long as we remain true to the gospel of Jesus Christ, just as they did.

Chapter 9

What Do We Believe?
(and Why Does It Matter?)

Our family tree helps define who we are as United Methodists. We also need to understand what we are. What do we believe, and why does it matter? First of all, as Christians, we hold some beliefs in common with all Christians.

We believe in the One God: Father, Son, and Holy Spirit. We believe that God is alive and active in the world, that Jesus Christ is Lord and Savior, and that the Holy Spirit dwells within us as our guide. Many churches sing about the Trinity every Sunday when they sing the Doxology. Here is one version that appears in *The United Methodist Hymnal* (94): "Praise God, the source of all our gifts! Praise Jesus Christ, whose power uplifts! Praise the Spirit, Holy Spirit!"

We believe that every person is a sinner who needs God's salvation. We believe that salvation and redemption come through faith in Jesus Christ, not through anything that we do ourselves. We believe that all those who put their trust in Jesus are made new. One of the best-known hymns of the church, written by Charles Wesley, describes what we think about Jesus: "O for a thousand tongues to sing my great Redeemer's praise." Wesley writes about a Jesus whose name is "music in the sinner's ears," whose love sets us free, whose blood was shed for each of us. Because of Jesus, we can "feel [our] sins forgiven" (the *Hymnal,* 57).

We believe that Christ will come again, and that God's work in the world will be fulfilled with Christ's return. The African American spiritual "My Lord, What a Morning" (719) invites us to sing of this hope in Christ's return: "My Lord, what a morning, when the stars begin to fall. You'll hear the trumpet sound, . . . You'll hear the sinner moan, . . . You'll hear the Christian shout."

We believe in the power of Scripture as the rule and guide for our lives.

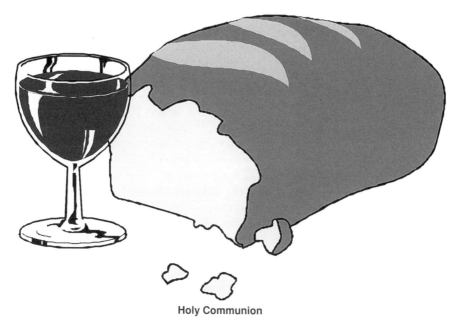

Holy Communion

As the hymn says, the words of the Bible are "wonderful words of life" (600). We believe that we are part of Christ's universal church with all fellow believers. With other Christians, we believe that Holy Communion and baptism are sacraments, ways in which God's grace is received. The hymn "One Bread, One Body" (620) describes how the sacrament of Communion symbolizes our unity with all Christians everywhere: "One bread, one body, one Lord of all, one cup of blessing which we bless. And we, though many throughout the earth, we are one body in this one Lord."

These beliefs, held in common with other Christians all over the world, are the foundation of our faith. They give structure and meaning to our lives. They help us understand who God is and how God works. They also help us understand who we are, both sinners in need of God's grace and greatly beloved children of God. The beliefs help us know what our priorities ought to be, and how we can act as God's people in the world. In times of trouble, confusion, or sorrow, they comfort and strengthen us.

There are other beliefs that are Methodism's special contribution to the

Christian faith. United Methodists believe in prevenient grace, or the love of God that surrounds us even before we are aware of it. If you think about taking care of a baby, you can begin to understand this idea. A baby doesn't think about where her care is coming from. She just expects that she will be fed and clothed and changed and cuddled. In the same way, God pours blessings on people who don't know who the Giver is. Just as a baby who has been loved grows up to be a loving child, so does prevenient grace help prepare a person's heart for the transforming love of God.

United Methodists believe that any person can be transformed by the love of God. Salvation is not limited to a chosen few. We use the term *conversion* to describe this process of transformation. Sometimes it happens suddenly (there are many people who can name the exact day and the exact time when they turned their lives over to Christ). For others it's a more gradual process, a growth in God's love without a specific dramatic turning point. This transformation is a free gift of God; there is nothing we can do to earn or deserve it. As John Wesley put it, "The grace or love of God, whence cometh our salvation, is free in all, and free for all" (from Sermon 110, "Free Grace"[1739], in *The Works of John Wesley* [Bicentennial Edition], Volume 3; Abingdon Press, 1986; page 544).

United Methodists believe that we can feel an inner assurance that God's love has saved us from our sins, just as Wesley did in the meeting at Aldersgate Street. Remember what he said? "I felt my heart strangely warmed. I felt I did trust in Christ, Christ alone for salvation; and an assurance was given me that He had taken away *my* sins, even *mine*, and saved *me* from the law of sin and death."

United Methodists believe that salvation is not the end of our spiritual journey. In fact, in many ways, it's just the beginning. We believe that we are "going on to perfection," that we can be "sanctified," made perfect in love. This doesn't mean that we become perfect people, never making a mistake or sinning. Rather it means that we believe that a person can be so completely filled with the love of God that she or he does not consciously commit a sin. It is as if we can become so preoccupied, so focused on living a holy life, on walking the Christian way, that no sinful thoughts or actions have room to grow in our hearts. It's like a flower garden that is so carefully tended that the weeds just never have a place to grow.

United Methodists believe in the importance of holy living. If we are

Christians, we will try to live our lives so that all of our actions, all of our decisions, reflect our devotion to God. We make our faith active, doing good works as a reflection of our love for God and God's love for us. Part of putting our faith into action is to get involved in Christian mission and service, whether that's fixing roofs, singing at a nursing home, or writing letters in support of a cause close to one's heart. The source of any holiness in our lives is God, not our own actions.

United Methodists acknowledge that accepting God's love and salvation in Christ is not a lifetime guarantee that a person will never drift away from God. As Wesley said, "There is no such height or strength of holiness as it is impossible to fall from" (from "A Plain Account of Christian Perfection," in *The Works of the Rev. John Wesley*, Volume XI; Wesleyan-Methodist Book-Room, 1872; page 426). This realization means that it takes constant vigilance and work to be a Christian. The decision to follow Christ must be made over and over again, as we pursue our daily lives. The Christian walk is a marvelous, challenging thing; but we have to keep paying attention so that we don't wander down blind alleys or get distracted by worldly values along the way.

How do we stay on the Christian path? United Methodists believe that one of the best things we can do is to spend time with other Christians. John Wesley said, "The gospel of Christ knows of no religion, but social; no holiness but social holiness" (from "Preface to Hymns and Sacred Poems" [1739], in *The Works of John Wesley,* Volume XIV; Zondervan, 1959; page 321). Living a Christian life is hard if we isolate ourselves from other people. Other Christians in a worshiping community are vital to our spiritual growth. The organization of The United Methodist Church is designed to keep all of us connected. We have what we call a "connectional" system. Each local church belongs to a district that includes other churches in the vicinity. Several districts make up an annual conference. The annual conferences connect with one another through general church agencies.

More important, within the local church there are many places to connect with other believers—at worship, in Sunday school and youth group, in choirs, and in Bible studies, just to name a few. These small groups can strengthen one's faith by maintaining a connection with another Christians. In the words of the old hymn, "Blest be the tie that binds our hearts in Christian love; the fellowship of kindred minds is like to that above" (557).

United Methodists believe that we are to practice our faith in a disciplined way. Our faith—our assurance of God's love and of our salvation in Jesus Christ—is like a beautiful instrument that we have been given as a free gift. This amazing gift is nothing we bought for ourselves or earned by being such good musicians. But if we don't practice that instrument, we will become rusty and will not get the full benefit out of having it. If we practice, we will become better and better musicians; and the music we play will bring us and others great joy. We can't just practice a few minutes once or twice a week, however; these deliberate efforts have to be an essential, central part of our lives every single day.

Chapter 10

How Do We Practice Our Faith?

Imagine that someone has given you a beautiful musical instrument—a violin, or piano, or guitar. What will you do with it? Will you learn to play it, or will you put it in the corner and ignore it?

The Christian faith is a little like that musical instrument. A free gift from a loving God, our faith is ours to develop or ignore. Why would anyone ignore a gift from God? For one thing, if you have ever played an instrument, you know that it takes a lot of practice before you can play well. It takes commitment, the willingness to hone your skills day after day, even when the task seems hard, or boring, or irrelevant.

And what do you get for all that practice? An abiding appreciation of music's power and beauty is one major benefit. Perhaps the most rewarding result is an ability to communicate with others in a language that speaks directly from the heart. The same thing happens when we practice our faith. We develop the ability to see God at work, to trust in God for everything, and to communicate God's love to everyone we meet.

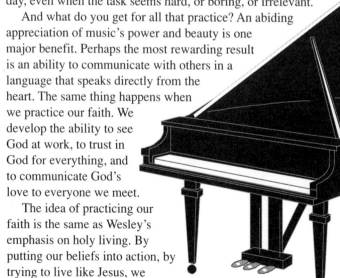

The idea of practicing our faith is the same as Wesley's emphasis on holy living. By putting our beliefs into action, by trying to live like Jesus, we practice our faith. And we have tools to help us: The Bible's teachings are the foundation of our faith. Then we have the beliefs that we talked about in the previous chapter. We also have the witness of fellow Christians, from the earliest days of the church up through the witness of present-day Christians, from the apostle Paul to Susanna Wesley, from Harry Hosier to Mother Teresa. There are probably people in your own life who are models of Christian faith for you— relatives, friends, teachers. Seeing how they respond to challenges in their lives can help you when you face your own challenges.

United Methodists emphasize the idea of community and connection because we believe that it's easier to practice our faith when we have others to help us. In the early years of John Wesley's ministry, his followers gathered into regular groups that Wesley called "societies." In today's language we might call them fellowship groups or discipleship teams. These groups were made up of people who were seeking to know and follow God, and who had responded to the Wesleyan message of salvation and holy living. As Wesley phrased it, the only membership requirement for the Methodist societies was a desire to be saved from one's sins.

Wesley and his preachers soon discovered that the members of the societies needed some guidance. Although they wanted to follow God, they were sometimes unclear about how to do it. Wesley kept preaching the message that when we focus our attention on God, we must change everything in our lives that is not pleasing to God. Wesley noticed that some members of the societies frequently got drunk, lied, gossiped, got into fist fights, swore, and did other things that couldn't exactly be called "holy living."

So Wesley divided each society (which might have hundreds of members) into smaller groups called "classes" of about twelve people each. Every class had a specially trained leader. Wesley wanted these classes to be a place where people could talk about the intimate details of their Christian walk—what their struggles and temptations were, what they were learning, and where they needed help and support.

In order to help the societies understand what he meant by holy living, Wesley drew up a set of rules for society members to follow. In presenting these "General Rules" to the societies, he stressed that no one had to do anything special to join the societies. But to stay in the society, a member's life had to bear the fruit of holy living. Wesley identified three major ways that others can judge whether someone is truly living a holy life:

► First, the holy person does "no harm" to others and avoids evil of every kind.
► Second, the holy person actively does good to everyone he or she meets.
► Third, the holy person "[attends] upon all the ordinances of God."

Wesley included a list of specific practices and behaviors that Methodists thought were evil. In some ways they reflect the time in which Wesley lived, but many of them still concern us today. The General Rules named as evil the use of profanity and said it is wrong to treat Sunday like any other working day, instead of a special day set aside by God for worship and rest.

Many of the evils that Wesley named are behaviors that affect other people, like drunkenness, fighting, getting back at someone who has harmed you (instead of forgiving and forgetting), or treating others in ways you wouldn't want to be treated. He didn't want people speaking unkindly about others, or Christian brothers and sisters taking one another to court. When the General Rules were adopted by the new American church some years later, the Americans added another evil to the list: slaveholding and the buying and selling of slaves.

Wesley also felt that the way people spend their money is part of holy living. He didn't want the members of the societies borrowing or lending money at a high rate of interest (called "usury") or buying something if they knew they couldn't pay for it. He said Methodists shouldn't waste their money on expensive clothes or jewelry. In fact, Methodists became well known, and sometimes ridiculed, for their plain and simple clothing. Wesley in turn reminded his followers that Jesus told us not to "store up . . . treasures on earth" (Matthew 6:19).

Finally, the way believers spend their free time is also an important part of holy living. The General Rules warned society members that it is wrong to be lazy and self-indulgent, and to waste time on amusements that don't glorify God.

That's quite a list of "Don'ts!" Wesley's second General Rule talks about some "Do's." Simply put, he wanted his followers to do good to all they met, anytime and anywhere, with no thought for themselves. They should take care of people's physical needs, by feeding the hungry, giving clothing to the needy, and helping those who are ill or in prison. They should also be

mindful of people's spiritual needs, by talking about God's love to everyone they encounter and teaching others about the Christian way.

Wesley wanted his followers to look out for one another. He thought Christians should patronize other Christian businesses, hire other Christians to work for them, and generally help one another along in the world.

He wanted society members to work diligently and live frugally, so that all the world would see what kind of people Christians were. Finally, he reminded his followers of Paul's words, that as Christians they should run with patience the race that is set before them. They shouldn't complain about their lives, but recognize that God has placed them where they are for a reason. They shouldn't worry about the world's opinion of them, or about their status in the world, remembering that when they are criticized or ridiculed, it is all for the Lord's sake. Indeed, they should expect to be unpopular in the world; for they are following the One who has overcome the world and whose teachings go against everything that the world thinks is important or valuable.

Wesley's third General Rule pertains to the Christian's involvement in the church. He taught that an important proof of the Christian life of holiness is active participation in the life of the church, what he called "the ordinances of God." These "ordinances" included going to church on Sundays and at other times of public worship (not just going to the society meetings), participating in the Lord's Supper, praying in private and with other Christians, reading and studying the Bible, and fasting.

As you can see, Wesley's rules for his followers covered just about everything. To Wesley and the early Methodists, each part of our life, from how we spend our money to the way we treat others to what we do for fun, should reflect our commitment to Christ. Our faith should in no way be just a Sunday-morning thing. We are accountable as Christians for every single aspect of our life.

To return to our musical image, just as practicing a musical instrument makes a person a better musician, when the Christian actively practices the instrument of faith, his or her heart becomes more and more filled with love, so that the "Do's" and "Don'ts" of holy living become more natural.

By listing such specific examples, did Wesley mean to say that these are the only good behaviors and evil actions to think about? Certainly not. Did he mean that anyone who slips up on any of these things isn't a Christian? Certainly not. Rather, he gave specific examples that the people of his day could directly relate to, as suggestions for actively practicing holy living in their real life. And then, just as now, Christians found it difficult to toe the line all the time.

Methodists wrote Wesley letters about how difficult it was to keep all the rules. One follower, Thomas Willis, wrote him a long, sincere letter describing how he tried to keep all the rules, but couldn't do it perfectly. He particularly mentioned the prohibition Wesley had placed on buying and selling on Sunday. Willis was a farmer, and said he thought that selling milk on Sunday mornings was "work of necessity and mercy." He reminded Wesley that "the laws of the nation do allow selling milk on Sunday mornings. The cows must be milked on Sundays; children must be fed with the milk, and if it is not used it will not keep good from Sunday morning till Monday." (This, of course, was in the days before refrigeration.) Wesley recognized the truth of Willis' words, and wrote "Quite right" in the margin of the letter. Now, Wesley did not remove the prohibition; but he recognized that people were living in the real world, and that the true goal, as Thomas Willis put it about himself, was that "through the grace which God hath bestowed upon me my whole desire and the bent of my heart is, that whether I eat or drink, or whatsoever I do, I may do it all to the glory of God" (from letter from Thomas Willis to John Wesley, Nov. 13, 1744, in *The Works of John Wesley*, Volume 26, edited by Frank Baker; Oxford University Press, 1982; page 116).

Put in their simplest terms, the General Rules tell us to do good, not evil. They tell us that the Christian's life should reflect God's love in every single area, from the way we treat the check-out clerk at the grocery store to the amount of money we spend on our clothes. They tell us that it is important to pay attention to anything, large or small, that may be keeping us from living out our faith, that may be preventing us from being truly close to God and understanding God's will for our lives.

Wesley's Rules were designed to be put into practice in a community of faith. Ideally, the members of the society in their smaller "clases" would develop relationships of trust and caring, where people could honestly communicate with others and be open to others' guidance and even criticism. The whole goal was to work together in love so that God's love could be seen in the lives of the people called Methodists.

The General Rules have guided our church from its beginning, especially because they have always reminded us that our goal is to live holy lives. Other guidance for living a holy life comes from the church's Social Principles, which help us understand how to live out our personal faith in the world—through mission, in service, and by speaking out on issues that affect people's physical and spiritual well-being.

In some ways, the General Rules were the Social Principles of the early Methodist movement; for they stressed Methodists' responsibility to care for the body as well as the spirit. They recognized that Christians live in the world and stressed that their lives must be a witness in the world. As we saw earlier, the first modern expression of concern for justice in the world was the Social Creed, adopted by The Methodist Episcopal Church in 1908. Other predecessors of The United Methodist Church (The Methodist Episcopal Church, South; The Methodist Protestant Church; and The Evangelical United Brethren Church) also adopted similar statements.

In 1972, four years after the creation of The United Methodist Church, the General Conference adopted a new statement of Social Principles. Every four years, at General Conference, the church, through its elected delegates, can update the language and discuss changes in the Principles. The Social Principles are the church's opportunity to speak with one voice on issues that affect human beings, from nuclear proliferation and environmental pollution to abortion and homosexual rights. Because our church is so diverse, it can be difficult for hundreds of delegates to General Conference to speak with one voice; but sometimes in the discussions and even in the arguments people come to a new understanding and find words that can speak for all.

How do the Social Principles help us practice our faith as United Methodist Christians? By addressing such a wide variety of issues, they help us to see that as Christians we are called to respond to the world, to deal with complicated issues, and to take a stand instead of hiding our heads in the sand. By expressing the church's stand on these issues, they give each of us a place to start. Will every United Methodist agree with every sentence in the Social Principles? By no means! They are, however, a starting point for discussion and understanding. By making a public statement about issues affecting all human beings, the Social Principles show that The United Methodist Church stands as a witness to the truth of the gospel and in the line of our Wesleyan heritage of holy living.

Who are United Methodists? What do we believe? How do we live out our beliefs? We hope this study has helped you answer those questions, with stories from our collective past and thoughts about our current church life. The big challenge for you, for all of us, is in recognizing that what we do today as United Methodists will provide new answers to those questions for all those who will come after us. We stand on a strong foundation; now it's our turn to build.

Index

Selected Bibliography

Barclay. Wade C. *History of Methodist Missions.* 4 vols. New York: Board of Missions, The Methodist Church, 1949–1957.

Behney, J. Bruce, and Paul H. Eller. *The History of the Evangelical United Brethren Church.* Nashville: Abingdon, 1979.

Bordin, Ruth. *Frances Willard: A Biography.* Chapel Hill, N.C: University of North Carolina Press, 1986.

Brailsford, Mabel R. *A Tale of Two Brothers: John and Charles Wesley.* London: Rupert Hart-Davis, 1954.

Bucke, Emory S., ed. *History of American Methodism.* 3 vols. Nashville: Abingdon Press, 1964.

Edwards, Maldwyn. *Family Circle: A Study of the Epworth Household in Relation to John and Charles Wesley.* London: Epworth Press, 1949.

Green, V.H.H. *John Wesley.* Lanham, MD: University Press of America, 1987.

Heitzenrater, Richard P. *Wesley and the People Called Methodists.* Nashville: Abingdon Press, 1995.

McElhenney, John G., ed. *United Methodism in America: A Compact History.* Nashville: Abingdon Press, 1992.

Norwood, Frederick A. *Sourcebook of American Methodism.* Nashville: Abingdon Press, 1983.

Norwood, Frederick A. *The Story of American Methodism: A History of the United Methodists and Their Relations.* Nashville: Abingdon Press, 1974.

O'Malley, J. Steven. *Pilgrimage of Faith: The Legacy of the Otterbeins.* Metuchen, NJ: Scarecrow Press, 1973.

Rack, Henry D. *Reasonable Enthusiast: John Wesley and the Rise of Methodism.* London: Epworth Press, 1989.

Rudolph, L.C. *Francis Asbury.* Nashville: Abingdon Press, 1983.

Sangrey, Abram. W. *Martin Boehm, Pioneer Preacher in the Christian Faith and Practice.* [S.1., s.n.], © 1976 (Ephrata, PA: Science Press).

Smith, Warren T. *Harry Hosier, Circuit Rider.* Nashville: Discipleship Resources, 1981.

Vickers, John A. *Francis Asbury.* Peterborough [England]: Foundery Press, 1993.

Wilson, Robert S. *Jacob Albright: The Evangelical Pioneer.* Myerstown, PA: Church Center Press of Evangelical Congregational Church, 1940.